W9-CUE-954

Follow the Map

Every Vitamix machine is designed to perform more than 10 different culinary techniques, which the following recipes will help you master. Here's a quick guide to help you follow our map, until you're ready to go off-recipe.

Program Settings

If your machine has program settings, you can look for the program icons located next to recipe titles. Simply load the container and select the correct program. The blender will process your recipe and turn off automatically.

Smoothies: A 45-second blend for silky smooth, whole-food beverages

Frozen Desserts: A 55-second blend for refreshing sorbets, frozen yogurts, and granitas

Hot Soups: A 6-minute 30-second blend designed to heat raw ingredients to steaming hot soups, simply using the friction of the blades

Dips + Spreads: A 1-minute blend for smooth hummus, baby food, and more

Family of Containers

Our complete line of Self-Detect containers is designed to let you blend just the right amount and quickly serve, store, or take food to go.

All recipes in this book are created for the 64-ounce container, but the 48-ounce container can also be used at times. Look for container icons at the top of each recipe to know which is recommended for the task at hand. You can purchase additional containers (also available in 32-, 20-, and 8-ounce sizes) and find accompanying recipes at **vitamix.com.**

64 Low-Profile 64-ounce Container

48 48-ounce Container

Join Our Community

Visit **vitamix.com/community** to explore
others' culinary adventures + link to our
social pages, where you can share your
own creations using **#Vitamix**.

There's Always More to Explore

Our culinary team is always
tinkering with something new. Find
hundreds of recipes, additional cookbooks,
+ container accessories at **vitamix.com**.

Beverages

Back in the 80s when hair was big, everything was a 'Rainbow Connection', and parachutes were actually pants, Grandpa Barnard coined the smoothie, Kick-a-poo Joy Juice during demonstrations. It took some persuasion to get the first customer to give the original vegetable drink a try, but in short order, the eager line formed and the rest is history.

Robin Dieterich,
Archivist

Fifth generation

Beverages

10	Avocado, Cucumber + Lime Smoothie
10	Apple Kale Smoothie
10	Hint of Mint Smoothie
10	Spring Green Smoothie
15	Honey Kombucha Smoothie
15	Cinnamon Date Fruit Smoothie
16	Açai Bowl
16	Berry Cherry Breakfast Bowl
19	Almond Milk
19	Cashew Milk
21	Basil Lemonade
21	Apple Beet Juice
21	Citrus Carrot Juice
22	Whole Fruit Margarita
22	Cider + Whiskey Cocktail
22	Pomarita
25	Mocha Spiced Coffee
25	Banana Cream Pie Milkshake

Design Your Own Smoothie

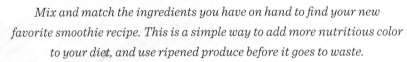

Mix and match the ingredients you have on hand to find your new favorite smoothie recipe. This is a simple way to add more nutritious color to your diet, and use ripened produce before it goes to waste.

I used to spend $5-$8 on smoothies and now I make my own! This is the exact blender the juice bar at our local health food store uses!"

–Annied732, NJ

01.

Choose 1 Liquid:

1 cup soy milk

1 cup yogurt

1 cup fruit juice

1 cup water

Blend.

Place your
ingredients and 1
cup ice cubes into
the container in the
order recommended
and secure the lid.

Select Variable
1 or the Smoothie
setting.

Start the machine,
slowly increase to its
highest speed, and
blend for 45 seconds;
or start the machine
and allow the
Smoothie program
to complete.

02.

Choose 2 Fruits + Vegetables:

1 apple

1 cup strawberries

1 cup blueberries

1 cup grapes

1 orange, peeled

1 cup melon, peeled

1 cup pineapple

1 banana, peeled

1 carrot

1 cup peaches

1 cup mango, peeled

½ cup papaya, peeled

1 pear

2 stalks celery

1 kiwi, peeled

½ cup cucumber

03.

Choose 1 Green:
(optional)

2 cups spinach

1 cup kale

½ head of romaine

1 romaine heart

¾ cup raw broccoli

1 small head of Bibb
or Boston lettuce

*

When you
combine blue
fruits with
greens, the
resulting color
is somewhere in
the brown family,
so add blues in
small quantities
to retain an
appetizing color.

Avocado, Cucumber + Lime Smoothie

64 **48** / *Serves 2* / *Total Time: 10 minutes*

2 Tablespoons fresh lime juice

4 Tablespoons water

1 teaspoon fresh lime zest

2 cups (240 g) chopped cucumber

½ ripe avocado (30 g), peeled

⅛ teaspoon ground black pepper

1 cup (130 g) ice cubes

Amount Per 1 Cup (240 ml) Serving:
Calories 80, Total Fat 5g, Saturated Fat 1g, Cholesterol
0mg, Sodium 10mg, Total Carbohydrate 9g,
Dietary Fiber 3g, Sugars 2g, Protein 2g

Apple Kale Smoothie

64 **48** / *Serves 3* / *Total Time: 10 minutes*

½ cup (120 ml) water

1 cup (150 g) green grapes

½ orange, peeled and seeded

½ green apple, halved and seeded

2 cups (130 g) kale

2 cups (260 g) ice cubes

Amount Per 1 Cup (240 ml) Serving:
Calories 40, Total Fat 0g, Saturated Fat 0g, Cholesterol
0mg, Sodium 5mg, Total Carbohydrate 10g,
Dietary Fiber 1g, Sugars 8g, Protein 1g

Hint of Mint Smoothie

64 / *Serves 6* / *Total Time: 10 minutes*

1 cup (240 ml) water

1½ cups (240 g) green grapes

4½ cups (100 g) loosely packed spinach

6 to 8 fresh mint leaves

2½ cups (385 g) fresh pineapple chunks

1 cup (130 g) ice cubes

Amount Per 1 Cup (240 ml) Serving:
Calories 70, Total Fat 0g, Saturated Fat 0g, Cholesterol
0mg, Sodium 40mg, Total Carbohydrate 17g,
Dietary Fiber 1g, Sugars 12g, Protein 1g

Spring Green Smoothie

64 / *Serves 5* / *Total Time: 10 minutes*

¼ cup (60 ml) water

1½ cups (225 g) green grapes

1 orange, peeled and halved

½ lemon, peeled

½ cucumber, rough chopped

½ green apple (100 g), halved and seeded

1 cup (65 g) kale

1 cup (50 g) spring greens mix

1 cup (60 g) fresh parsley leaves

1 cup (150 g) frozen pineapple chunks

2 cups (260 g) ice cubes

Amount Per 1 Cup (240 ml) Serving:
Calories 90, Total Fat 0g, Saturated Fat 0g, Cholesterol
0mg, Sodium 10mg, Total Carbohydrate 22g,
Dietary Fiber 3g, Sugars 13g, Protein 2g

*
Instructions

Add all ingredients to
the Vitamix container
in the order listed and
secure the lid. Select
Variable 1 or the
Smoothie program.
Start the machine,
slowly increase to
its highest speed,
and blend for 45
seconds; or start the
machine and allow
the Smoothie
program to complete.

Matcha

Benefits /
antioxidants, Vitamin C

Flavor profile /
green tea

Use as /
a complement to
mint, citrus, or coffee-
flavored drinks

Kombucha

Benefits / probiotic

Flavor profile /
sweetened vinegar

Use as /
a replacement
for water or juice,
starting in small
quantities

Superfood
Smoothie Boosters

*When you're ready to kick your smoothie nutrition
up a notch, here are a few ingredients to try.*

Cacao

Benefits / antioxidants,
many essential vitamins
and minerals

Flavor profile /
resembles the bitter-
sweetness of dark
chocolate

Use as / a healthy
boost to fruit smoothies
and sorbets

per 8-ounce
smoothie

Kombucha: 1/4 cup
Matcha: 1 teaspoon
Cacao: 1 Tablespoon
Flax: 1 Tablespoon
Kefir: 1/2 cup
Chia: 1 Tablespoon
Açai: 1 teaspoon
Goji Berries: 1/4 cup

Flax

Benefits /
omega-3 fatty
acids, antioxidants,
Vitamin B1,
dietary fiber

Flavor profile /
nutty

Use as /
a balance
to sweeter fruits
and vegetables

Açai

Benefits /
antioxidants, fiber,
healthy fats

Flavor profile /
sweet and tart,
like raspberry

Use as /
a sweetener
in smoothies and
smoothie bowls

Kefir

Benefits / probiotic,
protein, calcium

Flavor profile /
slightly sour, like
plain yogurt

Use as /
a replacement
for milk or yogurt

Goji Berries

Benefits / vitamins,
antioxidants

Flavor profile /
slightly bitter, like
cranberry

Use as /
a replacement
for tart red berries

Chia

Benefits /
calcium, protein

Flavor profile /
flavorless

Use as / recipe
thickener; soak in
water before adding
to the container

> "I can easily get leafy greens in my young children by adding the greens to smoothies.
>
> —EmBYU, Michigan

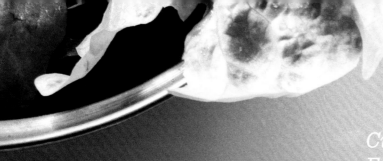

Honey Kombucha Smoothie

64 **48** / *Serves 3*
Total Time: 10 minutes

1¼ cups (300 ml) ginger kombucha

2 Tablespoons (30 ml) lemon juice

3 Tablespoons (45 ml) honey

1 cup (125 g) frozen mango chunks, thawed

½ frozen banana (45 g)

1 cup (120 g) frozen blackberries

Add all ingredients to the Vitamix container in the order listed and secure the lid. Select Variable 1, start the machine, and slowly increase to its highest speed. Blend for 1 minute 15 seconds.

Amount Per 1 Cup (240 ml) Serving:
Calories 150, Total Fat 0g, Saturated Fat 0g, Cholesterol 0mg, Sodium 5mg, Total Carbohydrate 39g, Dietary Fiber 3g, Sugars 30g, Protein 1g

Cinnamon Date Fruit Smoothie

64 **48** / *Serves 4*
Total Time: 10 minutes

---

1 cup water (240 ml)

2 ripe bananas, peeled

½ teaspoon cinnamon

½ teaspoon vanilla

½ cup (70 g) dried pitted dates

1 cup (130 g) frozen cherries

1 cup (130 g) ice cubes

Add all ingredients to the Vitamix container in the order listed and secure the lid. Select Variable 1, start the machine, and slowly increase to its highest speed. Blend for 1 minute.

Amount Per 1 Cup (240 ml) Serving:
Calories 130, Total Fat 0g, Saturated Fat 0g, Cholesterol 0mg, Sodium 5mg, Total Carbohydrate 32g, Dietary Fiber 2g, Sugars 12g, Protein 2g

Açai Bowl

 64 48 / *Serves 2* / *Total Time: 10 minutes*

½ cup (120 ml) apple juice

1½ cups (215 g) frozen blueberries

1 frozen Sambazon Açai Bar, broken into 4 pieces

1½ frozen bananas (165 g), sliced

3 cups (60 g) kale

¼ teaspoon matcha green tea powder

Garnish: Granola and sweetened
shaved coconut

Amount Per 1 Cup (240 ml) Serving: Calories 230,
Total Fat 4.5g, Saturated Fat 1.5g, Cholesterol 0mg, Sodium 25mg,
Total Carbohydrate 50g, Dietary Fiber 7g, Sugars 33g, Protein 3g

Berry Cherry Breakfast Bowl

 64 / *Serves 3* / *Total Time: 15 minutes*

½ cup (120 ml) almond milk

½ Tablespoon açai powder

6 blackberries (30 g)

6 pitted cherries (45 g)

1 ripe banana, peeled

2 cups (250 g) ice cubes

2½ cups (285 g) frozen strawberries

Garnish: Granola, fresh
blueberries, drizzle of honey

Amount Per 1 Cup (240 ml) Serving: Calories 150, Total
Fat 6g, Saturated Fat 3g, Cholesterol 0mg, Sodium 50mg, Total
Carbohydrate 26g, Dietary Fiber 7g, Sugars 11g, Protein 5g

✳

Instructions

Add all smoothie
bowl ingredients
to the Vitamix
container in the
order listed and
secure the lid.
Select Variable 1,
start the machine,
and slowly increase
to its highest
speed. Blend for
45 seconds to 1
minute, using the
tamper to press
ingredients toward
the blades. Garnish.

The Perfect Smoothie Bowl

If you'd rather spoon than slurp, you can tweak any smoothie recipe to convert it to a bowl. Simply reduce the liquid to about ⅓ cup, swap frozen fruit for fresh, and add a thickening protein, like one from the list below.

Thickeners: nut butter, tofu, Greek yogurt, chia, avocado.

*Dairy
Substitution
Guide*

1 cup buttermilk =
1 cup almond milk +
1 Tablespoon lemon juice

1 cup butter =
1 1/2 cups olive oil

1 Tablespoon butter =
2 1/2 teaspoons olive oil

1 cup sour cream =
1 cup soy yogurt

1 cup yogurt =
1/2 cup coconut milk +
1/2 cup applesauce

Almond Milk

 / *Serves 4*
Total Time: 12 hours

1 cup (135 g) raw, blanched almonds, covered in cold water and soaked overnight

3 cups (720 ml) water

½ teaspoon pure vanilla extract, or 1 teaspoon pure maple syrup, optional

Add 3 cups of water, drained almonds, and sweetener to the Vitamix container in the order listed and secure the lid. Select Variable 1, start the machine, and slowly increase to its highest speed. Blend for 1 minute.

Amount Per 1 Cup (240 ml)
Serving: Calories 180, Total Fat 16g, Saturated Fat 1g, Cholesterol 0mg, Sodium 5mg, Total Carbohydrate 7g, Dietary Fiber 4g, Sugars 1g, Protein 7g

Cashew Milk

64 48 / *Serves 4*
Total Time: 12 hours

2 cups (250 g) roasted unsalted cashews, covered in water and soaked overnight

2 cups water (480 ml) (include soaking water plus enough to make 2 cups)

1 Tablespoon brown sugar

¼ teaspoon cinnamon

1 cup (130 g) ice cubes

Add all ingredients to the Vitamix container in the order listed and secure the lid. Select Variable 1, start the machine, and slowly increase to its highest speed. Blend for 40 seconds.

Amount Per 1 Cup (240 ml)
Serving: Calories 410, Total Fat 32g, Saturated Fat 6g, Cholesterol 0mg, Sodium 20mg, Total Carbohydrate 26g, Dietary Fiber 2g, Sugars 7g, Protein 10g

Benefits of
Whole-Food Juicing

In traditional juicing,
fruit and vegetable juice
is extracted from the
ingredient, leaving the
nutritious skin, pulp, and
fiber behind. Whole-food
(or raw) juicing uses the
entire ingredient to reduce
waste. The added fiber
keeps you fuller longer,
and provides a slower
release of sugar into
your bloodstream.

Basil Lemonade

(64) (48) / *Serves 4*
Total Time: 10 minutes

3 cups (720 ml) water

1½ lemons, peeled, halved, seeded

¼ cup (50 g) sugar or other sweetener

½ cup (20 g) fresh basil leaves

1 cup (130 g) ice cubes

Amount Per 1 Cup (240 ml) Serving:
Calories 80, Total Fat 0g, Saturated Fat 0g, Cholesterol 0mg, Sodium 5mg, Total Carbohydrate 22g, Dietary Fiber 1g, Sugars 20g, Protein 0g

Apple Beet Juice

(64) / *Serves 5*
Total Time: 10 minutes

1½ cups (360 ml) unsweetened apple juice

1¼ cups (35 g) spinach, loosely packed

3 cups (185 g) carrot, rough chopped

2 small raw beets (150 g) scrubbed, rough chopped

1 medium apple (150 g), seeded, cored and rough chopped

1¼ cups (160 g) ice cubes

Amount Per 1 Cup (240 ml) Serving:
Calories 80, Total Fat 0g, Saturated Fat 0g, Cholesterol 0mg, Sodium 65mg, Total Carbohydrate 20g, Dietary Fiber 3g, Sugars 14g, Protein 1g

Citrus Carrot Juice

(64) (48) / *Serves 4*
Total Time: 10 minutes

¾ cup (180 ml) water

2½ cups (410 g) fresh pineapple chunks

1 cup (165 g) chopped carrots

Slice of lemon, with peel

1½ cups (185 g) ice cubes

Amount Per 1 Cup (240 ml) Serving:
Calories 60, Total Fat 0g, Saturated Fat 0g, Cholesterol 0mg, Sodium 30mg, Total Carbohydrate 16g, Dietary Fiber 1g, Sugars 10g, Protein 1g

✳

Instructions

Add all ingredients to the Vitamix container in the order listed and secure the lid. Select Variable 1, start the machine, and slowly increase to its highest speed. Blend for 45 seconds.

Whole Fruit Margarita

64 **48** / *Serves 5*
Total Time: 10 minutes

¼ cup (60 ml) water

6 ounces (180 ml) tequila

2 ounces (60 ml) triple sec

1 medium orange, peeled, seeded, and halved

1 lime, peeled

1 lemon, peeled, seeded, and halved

6 Tablespoons (75 g) granulated sugar

6 cups (780 g) ice cubes

Amount Per 1 Cup (240 ml) Serving:
Calories 175 , Total Fat 0g, Saturated Fat 0g, Cholesterol 0mg, Sodium 1mg, Total Carbohydrate 20g, Dietary Fiber 1g, Sugars 18g, Protein 0g

Cider + Whiskey Cocktail

64 **48** / *Serves 3*
Total Time: 10 minutes

1 cup (240 ml) apple cider

4 ounces (120 ml) bourbon whiskey

2 Tablespoons (30 ml) maple syrup

½ small lemon, peeled and seeded

2 cups (260 g) ice cubes

Amount Per 1 Cup (240 ml) Serving:
Calories 140, Total Fat 0g, Saturated Fat 0g, Cholesterol 0mg, Sodium 10mg, Total Carbohydrate 17g, Dietary Fiber 0g, Sugars 15g, Protein 0g

Pomarita

64 **48** / *Serves 3*
Total Time: 10 minutes

½ cup (120 ml) tequila

1 cup (240 ml) 100% pomegranate juice

¼ cup (60 ml) triple sec

½ lime, peeled

2 cups (260 g) ice cubes

Amount Per 1 Cup (240 ml) Serving:
Calories 250, Total Fat 0g, Saturated Fat 0g, Cholesterol 0mg, Sodium 11mg, Total Carbohydrate 28g, Dietary Fiber 0g, Sugars 19g, Protein 1g

Instructions

Add all ingredients
to the Vitamix
container in the
order listed and
secure the lid.
Select Variable 1,
start the machine,
and slowly increase
to its highest
speed. Blend for
25 seconds.

Homemade Syrups

Design your own milkshakes, frozen coffees, and whipped creams by adding flavored syrups.

To make a basic simple syrup, combine equal parts of water and granulated sugar, simmer over medium heat until sugar is dissolved (about 10 minutes).

Add flavor by placing herbs and other ingredients into a separate container. When sugar has fully dissolved, pour syrup over herbs and flavorings. Let sit for two hours and cool to room temperature. Then simply use a fine mesh strainer and funnel to transfer into a glass bottle for storage. Here are some flavor combinations to get you started:

Salted Caramel:
drizzle of caramel syrup and a pinch of sea salt

Mint Chocolate Chip:
2 fresh mint sprigs and a small handful of chocolate chips

Chocolate Hazelnut:
1 Tablespoon each of hazelnuts and chocolate chips

Cinnamon:
½ stick of cinnamon

Mocha Spiced Coffee

 64 **48** / *Serves 2*
Total Time: 15 minutes

1½ cups (360 ml) milk

½ cup (90 g) semisweet chocolate chips

¼ teaspoon ground cinnamon

2 teaspoons instant espresso

⅛ teaspoon chili powder

Add all ingredients to the Vitamix container in the order listed and secure the lid. Select Variable 1, start the machine, and slowly increase to its highest speed. Blend for 5 minutes, or until heavy steam escapes from the vented lid.

Amount Per 1 Cup (240 ml) Serving:
Calories 320, Total Fat 19g, Saturated Fat 11g, Cholesterol 20mg, Sodium 90mg, Total Carbohydrate 37g, Dietary Fiber 3g, Sugars 32g, Protein 8g

Banana Cream Pie Milkshake

64 **48** / *Serves 3*
Total Time: 10 minutes

¼ cup plus 2 Tablespoons (90 ml) skim milk

3 cups (400 g) nonfat vanilla Greek frozen yogurt

1 banana, peeled

¼ cup plus 2 Tablespoons (30 g) graham cracker crumbs

Add all ingredients to the Vitamix container in the order listed and secure the lid. Select Variable 1, start the machine, and slowly increase speed to Variable 8. Blend for 40 seconds, using the tamper to press ingredients toward the blades.

Amount Per 1 Cup (240 ml) Serving:
Calories 290, Total Fat 1g, Saturated Fat 0g, Cholesterol 10mg, Sodium 190mg, Total Carbohydrate 53g, Dietary Fiber 1g, Sugars 48g, Protein 14g

Sauces, Dips + Spreads

I love cooking and couldn't wait to be allowed to use the Vitamix [blender] on my own. In my family, being able to drive that two horsepower motor is a rite of passage one must earn. My first mastery was the art of guacamole. It didn't take long before I was asked to bring it to every family outing, and my Aunt Beth dubbed me "Queen of the Guac."

Sydney Berg,
Fifth generation

Sauces, Dips + Spreads

"

*I make my famous
pasta sauce
from my garden
tomatoes and grate
the Parmesan and
Romano cheeses
for the pasta.*

–meiklem, Florida

Raw Tomato Sauce

64 / Serves 10
Total Time: 10 minutes

---

2 Tablespoons (30 ml) red wine vinegar

1½ pounds (670 g) plum tomatoes, halved

2 Tablespoons (20 g) Kalamata olives, pitted

⅓ cup (50 g) diced mozzarella cheese

1 garlic clove

2 teaspoons chopped fresh basil

2 teaspoons chopped fresh oregano

¼ teaspoon salt

2 Tablespoons (30 ml) extra virgin olive oil

Add vinegar, tomatoes, olives, cheese, garlic, herbs, and salt to the Vitamix container in the order listed and secure the lid. Select Variable 5. Pulse 12 times. Add oil. Select Variable 4 and Pulse 2 times. Transfer to a bowl and allow to sit until reaching room temperature, about 10 minutes.

Amount Per 1/4 Cup (60 ml)
Serving: Calories 35, Total Fat 3g, Saturated Fat 0.5g, Cholesterol 0mg, Sodium 80mg, Total Carbohydrate 2g, Dietary Fiber 1g, Sugars 1g, Protein 1g

Vegan Cheese Sauce

64 / Serves 12
Total Time: 15 minutes

---

2 cups (480 ml) water

¼ cup (60 ml) lemon juice

½ cup (100 g) canned pimentos, drained

1⅓ cups (140 g) whole raw almonds

2½ teaspoons onion powder

½ cup (60 g) nutritional yeast flakes

1 teaspoon kosher salt

Add all ingredients to the Vitamix container in the order listed and secure the lid. Select Variable 1, start the machine, and slowly increase to its highest speed. Blend for 3 minutes.

Amount Per 1/4 Cup (60 ml)
Serving: Calories 90, Total Fat 6g, Saturated Fat 0g, Cholesterol 0mg, Sodium 320mg, Total Carbohydrate 5g, Dietary Fiber 3g, Sugars 1g, Protein 5g

Kale + Basil Pesto

64 / Serves 16
Total Time: 10 minutes

---

1 cup olive oil

1 cup (100 g) grated Parmesan cheese

3 garlic cloves, peeled

2 cups (20 g) basil leaves

2 cups (35 g) kale leaves

3 Tablespoons pine nuts

¼ teaspoon salt

Pinch of ground black pepper

Add all ingredients to the Vitamix container in the order listed and secure the lid. Select Variable 1, start the machine, and slowly increase to its highest speed. Blend for 40 seconds.

Amount Per 2 Tablespoon (30 ml)
Serving: Calories 180, Total Fat 19g, Saturated Fat 3.5g, Cholesterol 5mg, Sodium 125mg, Total Carbohydrate 1g, Dietary Fiber 0g, Sugars 0g, Protein 3g

Herb
Flavor Profiles

Cilantro

Sprinkle fresh cilantro over Mexican and Vietnamese dishes. Heat can reduce its flavor, so add to the dish just before serving.

Lavender

Use sparingly in custard or ice cream to impart a subtle fragrance

Tarragon

Its slight licorice flavor can be challenging, but try in hollandaise, tomato sauces, and seafood.

Marjoram

A member of the mint family with a slight citrus flavor. Commonly used in Mediterranean dishes, sausage, and potatoes. Often paired with other spices, such as oregano, basil, and parsley.

Sage

Use to flavor butter or olive oil for light pasta dishes, or add to berry sauces for chicken, pork, or beef.

Rosemary

Most common to Italian meat and potato dishes. Add rosemary to a simple garlic butter sauce to flavor chicken and lamb.

Oregano

Use in Italian dishes like spaghetti and pizza sauces, as well as chili and vinaigrettes.

Basil

Available in a number of varieties, like opal basil (tomato salads), Thai basil (Thai and Vietnamese dishes), cinnamon or lemon basil (fruity desserts).

Traditional Hummus

/ *Serves 20* / *Total Time: 10 minutes*

2 (425 g) cans chickpeas, one drained, one with liquid

¼ cup (35 g) raw sesame seeds

1 Tablespoon olive oil

¼ cup (60 ml) lemon juice

¼ cup (60 ml) water

1 garlic clove, peeled

1 teaspoon ground cumin

½ teaspoon salt

Amount Per 2 Tablespoon (30 ml) Serving: Calories 35, Total Fat 1.5g, Saturated Fat 0g, Cholesterol 0mg, Sodium 125mg, Total Carbohydrate 5g, Dietary Fiber 1g, Sugars 0g, Protein 1g

Sweet + Spicy Beet Spread

64 48 / *Serves 24* / *Total Time: 30 minutes*

⅓ cup olive oil

2 Tablespoons honey

Juice and zest of 1 large lemon

¼ cup (60 ml) tahini

¼ cup white vinegar

1 large beet, roasted and peeled

1 (425 g) can chickpeas, drained

1 garlic clove, peeled

1 jalapeño pepper, seeded and quartered

¼ teaspoon sea salt

¼ teaspoon ground black pepper

Amount Per 2 Tablespoon (30 ml) Serving: Calories 80, Total Fat 5g, Saturated Fat 0.5g, Cholesterol 0mg, Sodium 80mg, Total Carbohydrate 7g, Dietary Fiber 0g, Sugars 2g, Protein 2g

Instructions

Add all ingredients to the Vitamix container in the order listed and secure the lid. Select Variable 1 or the Dips + Spreads program. Start the machine, slowly increase to its highest speed, and blend for 1 minute; or start the machine and allow the Dips + Spreads program to complete.

Guacamole

(64) / *Serves 16*
Total Time: 10 minutes

2 ripe avocados, peeled, pitted, and halved

1 Roma tomato, quartered

½ cup (10 g) fresh cilantro leaves

¼ cup (40 g) chopped red onion

2 Tablespoons (30 ml) lemon juice

½ teaspoon kosher salt

Add all ingredients to the Vitamix container in the order listed and secure the lid. Select Variable 4 and Pulse 5 to 6 times, using the tamper to press ingredients toward the blades.

Amount Per 2 Tablespoon (30 g) Serving: Calories 35, Total Fat 3g, Saturated Fat 0g, Cholesterol 0mg, Sodium 70mg, Total Carbohydrate 2g, Dietary Fiber 1g, Sugars 1g, Protein 0g

Tomatillo Pineapple Salsa

(64) / *Serves 10*
Total Time: 20 minutes

3 Tablespoons (45 ml) fresh orange juice

1½ Tablespoons fresh lime juice

1 Tablespoon white vinegar

3 fresh tomatillos (180 g), husked and quartered

⅓ cup (60 g) fresh pineapple chunks

⅓ cup (50 g) red onion, peeled and rough chopped

¼ cup (35 g) chopped red bell pepper

2 Tablespoons chopped fresh cilantro leaves

1 garlic clove, peeled

1½ teaspoons (10 g) seeded and chopped jalapeño

Add all ingredients to the Vitamix container in the order listed and secure the lid. Select Variable 4. Pulse 4 to 5 times, until desired consistency is reached.

Amount Per 2 Tablespoon (30 ml) Serving: Calories 10, Total Fat 0g, Saturated Fat 0g, Cholesterol 0mg, Sodium 0mg, Total Carbohydrate 3g, Dietary Fiber 0g, Sugars 2g, Protein 0g

California Salsa

(64) / *Serves 10*
Total Time: 15 minutes

½ medium onion, peeled and rough chopped

1 jalapeño pepper, seeds and membranes removed

¼ cup (5 g) chopped fresh cilantro leaves

Juice of ½ lemon or lime

½ teaspoon salt

6 ripe Roma tomatoes, quartered, divided use

Add onion, jalapeño, cilantro, juice, salt, and six of the tomato quarters to the Vitamix container in the order listed and secure the lid. Select Variable 5 and Pulse 5 times. Add the remaining tomato quarters through the lid plug opening. Pulse 10 to 12 times, or until desired consistency is reached.

Amount Per 1/4 Cup (60 g) Serving: Calories 11, Total Fat 0g, Saturated Fat 0g, Cholesterol 0mg, Sodium 142mg, Total Carbohydrate 3g, Dietary Fiber 1g, Sugars 0g, Protein 0g

Today I made
Paleo-approved
mayo. There are
plenty of recipes
and advice
to be found on
Facebook and
Pinterest
specifically for
Vitamix owners.

– Alary, Texas

Butter

---

3 cups (720 ml) whipping cream

¼ – ½ teaspoon kosher salt

Add cream to the Vitamix container and secure the lid. Select
Variable 1, start the machine, and slowly increase to its highest
speed. Blend for 1 minute, using the tamper to press the cream
toward the blades. Place in a fine strainer to drain any liquid.
Transfer to a bowl and add salt. Store in an airtight container.

Amount Per 1 Tablespoon (30 g) Serving:
Calories 100, Total Fat 11g, Saturated Fat 7g, Cholesterol 40mg, Sodium 30mg,
Total Carbohydrate 1g, Dietary Fiber 0g, Sugars 0g, Protein 1g

Homemade Mayonnaise

64 **48** / *Serves 28* / *Total Time: 10 minutes*

---

5 large egg yolks

3 Tablespoons fresh lemon juice

1½ teaspoons dry mustard

¼ teaspoon kosher salt

1 cup (240 ml) canola oil

Add yolks, lemon juice, mustard, and salt to the Vitamix
container in the order listed and secure the lid. Select Variable
1, start the machine, and slowly increase speed to Variable
5. Blend for 10 seconds. Reduce the speed to Variable 3 and
remove the lid plug. Slowly pour the oil through the lid plug
opening. Secure the lid plug and increase to the highest speed.
Blend for 15 to 20 seconds, or until emulsified.

Amount Per 1 Tablespoon (30 g) Serving:
Calories 100, Total Fat 11g, Saturated Fat 7g, Cholesterol 40mg, Sodium 30mg,
Total Carbohydrate 1g, Dietary Fiber 0g, Sugars 0g, Protein 1g

Artisanal Flavored Butters

Vitamix makes it
quick and easy to
make your own
homemade butters
to complement
breakfast, lunch, and
dinner. Experiment
with flavors by adding
spices and seasonings
in Step 1 of the
Vitamix butter recipe,
or by blending them
with unsalted butter
from the market.

Savory: rosemary,
basil, chives, cilantro,
dill, sage, lemongrass,
lemon thyme, or
lavender

Bold: Sun-dried
tomatoes, olives,
capers, peppadew
peppers, or
horseradish

Sweet: Honey,
molasses, maple
syrup, figs, prunes,
raisins, dates, dried
pineapple, mango, or
apricot

Spiced: Cinnamon,
nutmeg, allspice, or
garam masala

Memphis Barbecue Sauce

64 **48** / *Serves 20*
Total Time: 10 minutes

¼ cup (60 ml)
Worcestershire sauce

1½ cups (360 ml) white vinegar

¼ cup packed light
brown sugar (55 g)

2 Tablespoons onion powder

½ teaspoon salt

1 teaspoon ground black pepper

¼ teaspoon ground
cayenne pepper

¼ cup (60 ml) prepared
mustard (not Dijon-style)

2 cups (480 ml) ketchup

Add all ingredients to the
Vitamix container in the
order listed and secure the
lid. Select Variable 1, start the
machine, and slowly increase
to its highest speed. Blend for
45 seconds, or until desired
consistency is reached.

Amount Per 1/4 Cup (60 ml) Serving:
Calories 45, Total Fat 0g, Saturated Fat 0g,
Cholesterol 0mg, Sodium 390mg, Total
Carbohydrate 11g, Dietary Fiber 0g,
Sugars 9g, Protein 0g

Vegan Mayonnaise

64 **48** / *Serves 32*
Total Time: 10 minutes

¾ cup (180 ml) soy milk

1½ Tablespoons fresh lemon juice

1 teaspoon Dijon-style mustard

Pinch of salt

Pinch of ground black pepper

1 cup (240 ml) vegetable oil

Add milk, lemon juice, mustard, salt, and pepper to the Vitamix container in the order listed and secure the lid. Select Variable 1, start the machine, and slowly increase to its highest speed. Blend for 10 seconds. Reduce the speed to Variable 3 and remove the lid plug. Slowly pour the oil through the lid plug opening and secure the lid plug. Increase to highest speed and blend for 5 seconds.

Amount Per 1 Tablespoon (15 ml)
Serving: Calories 60, Total Fat 7g, Saturated Fat 0.5g, Cholesterol 0mg, Sodium 15mg, Total Carbohydrate 0g, Dietary Fiber 0g, Sugars 0g, Protein 0g

Avocado Hollandaise

64 / *Serves 24*
Total Time: 10 minutes

---

6 teaspoons fresh lemon juice

1½ very ripe, medium Haas avocados, peeled, pitted, and quartered

1½ cups (360 ml) hot water

¾ teaspoon salt

¾ teaspoon ground black pepper

6 Tablespoons (90 ml) vegetable oil

Add lemon juice, avocado, water, salt, and pepper to the Vitamix container in the order listed and secure the lid. Select Variable 1, start the machine, and increase to its highest speed. Blend for 30 seconds. Reduce the speed to Variable 5 and remove the lid plug. Slowly pour the oil through the lid plug opening. Secure the lid plug, slowly increase to highest speed, and blend for 15 seconds, or until desired consistency is reached.

Amount Per 2 Tablespoon (30 ml)
Serving: Calories 45, Total Fat 4.5g, Saturated Fat 0g, Cholesterol 0mg, Sodium 75mg, Total Carbohydrate 1g, Dietary Fiber 1g, Sugars 0g, Protein 0g

Nut Butters + Spreads

Homemade nut butters are a great way to add protein and healthy fats, without the added calories and preservatives of store-bought versions. Store them in the refrigerator for up to two weeks—there's no need to stir with each use.

Try these tips and ideas for creating your own customized nut butters at home.

01. Experiment with various combinations of nuts, including almonds, cashews, pecans, walnuts, pistachios, macadamia, or Brazil nuts. We recommend dry roasted for the richest flavor.

02. Add pumpkin, sunflower seeds, or soy nuts to the recipe for added nutrition.

03. Add sweetness with dried fruits like raisins or pitted dates, honey, maple syrup, vanilla, cocoa, cinnamon, or cardamom. Start small: A teaspoon of honey, ¼ teaspoon of cinnamon, for example. Sweetened nut butters are perfect on fresh fruit, blended into a smoothie, or spread on sandwich cookies.

04. Creamier consistencies can be created with a teaspoon of coconut oil for a subtle tropical flavor, or flaxseed oil for an omega 3 boost.

Peanut Butter

64 / *Serves 8*
Total Time: 5 minutes

4 cups (590 g) unsalted, dry roasted peanuts

Add nuts to the Vitamix container and secure the lid. Select Variable 1, start the machine, and slowly increase to its highest speed. Use the tamper to press ingredients toward the blades. In 1 minute, you will hear a high-pitched chugging sound. Once the butter begins to flow freely through the blades, reduce the speed to Variable 7. Blend for 30 seconds. Store refrigerated in an airtight container for up to one week.

Amount Per 1/4 Cup (60 ml)
Serving: Calories 210, Total Fat 18g, Saturated Fat 2.5g, Cholesterol 0mg, Sodium 0mg, Total Carbohydrate 8g, Dietary Fiber 3g, Sugars 2g, Protein 9g

Coconut Cashew Butter

64 48 / *Serves 8* / *Total Time: 10 minutes*

2 cups (210 g) roasted, salted cashews

½ cup (35 g) sweetened coconut flakes

2 Tablespoons (30 ml) agave

2 Tablespoons (30 ml) coconut oil

1 teaspoon coconut extract

1 cup (120 g) roasted peanuts

Add all ingredients to the Vitamix container in the order listed and secure the lid. Select Variable 1, start the machine, and slowly increase to its highest speed. Blend for 45 seconds, using the tamper to press ingredients toward the blades. Stop and scrape the sides of the container. Select Variable 1, start the machine, and slowly increase to its highest speed. Blend for 45 seconds, or until desired consistency is reached, using the tamper to press ingredients toward the blades.

Amount Per 1/4 Cup (60 ml) Serving: Calories 380, Total Fat 30g, Saturated Fat 9g, Cholesterol 0mg, Sodium 240mg, Total Carbohydrate 22g, Dietary Fiber 3g, Sugars 9g, Protein 10g

⁎

*Chocolate
Hazelnut Spread*

*1/4 cup dark chocolate chips
+ 2 cups hazelnuts*

2 cups (260 g) roasted sunflower seeds

¼ cup (40 g) flaxseed

¼ teaspoon salt, or to taste

Add all ingredients to the Vitamix container in the order listed and secure the lid. Select Variable 1, start the machine, and slowly increase to its highest speed. Blend for 45 seconds, using the tamper to press ingredients toward the blades. Stop and scrape the sides of the container. Select Variable 1, start the machine, and slowly increase to its highest speed. Blend for 15 to 30 seconds, or until desired consistency is reached, using the tamper to press ingredients toward the blades.

Amount Per 1/4 Cup (60 ml) Serving: : Calories 460, Total Fat 40g, Saturated Fat 4.5g, Cholesterol 0mg, Sodium 120mg, Total Carbohydrate 22g, Dietary Fiber 8g, Sugars 8g, Protein 11g

Soups, Salads + Dressings

Asparagus soup is one
of my 'go-to' recipes. Having
followed the recipe a million
times, I was surprised to
find one batch oddly gritty. It
wasn't until clean up that
I realized my mistake. The
grit in the soup was the well
ground remnants of the lid
to my jar of cashews.
Don't be afraid to make
mistakes—we all do!

Linda Barnard,
Third generation

Soups, Salads + Dressings

Cream of Asparagus Soup ☕

64 / *Serves 4*
Total Time: 30 minutes

1½ pounds (680 g) asparagus spears, cooked and cooled to room temperature (reserve one cup pieces for garnish)

1½ cups (360 ml) chicken broth

½ cup (120 ml) half & half

Salt, to taste

Ground black pepper, to taste

Add asparagus and chicken broth to the Vitamix container and secure the lid. Select Variable 1 or the Hot Soups program. Start the machine, slowly increase to its highest speed, and blend for 6 minutes 30 seconds; or start the machine and allow the Hot Soups program to complete. Select Variable 2, start the machine, and remove the lid plug. Add half & half through the lid plug opening. Blend for 10 seconds. Season to taste with salt and pepper and serve over reserved asparagus spears.

Amount Per 1 Cup (240 ml) Serving:
Calories 130, Total Fat 11g, Saturated Fat 6g, Cholesterol 35mg, Sodium 570mg, Total Carbohydrate 4g, Dietary Fiber 2g, Sugars 1g, Protein 6g

Carrot Potato Soup

64 / *Serves 8*
Total Time: 1 hour

1 Russet potato (145 g), peeled and quartered

1 large onion (75 g), peeled and quartered

4 carrots (150 g), scrubbed

7 cups (1.7 L) chicken or vegetable broth

Salt, to taste

Ground black pepper, to taste

Combine all ingredients in a large stock pot and cook over medium-high heat for 30 to 45 minutes, until the potatoes and carrots are tender. Carefully transfer the mixture from the stock pot into the Vitamix container and secure the lid. Select Variable 1, start the machine, and slowly increase to its highest speed. Blend for 2 minutes. Season to taste with salt and pepper.

Amount Per 1 Cup (240 ml) Serving:
Calories 80, Total Fat 0g, Saturated Fat 0g, Cholesterol 0mg, Sodium 230mg, Total Carbohydrate 18g, Dietary Fiber 2g, Sugars 5g, Protein 3g

Black Bean Soup

64 / Serves 5 / Total Time: 30 minutes

3 Tablespoons olive oil

½ cup (70 g) onions, rough chopped

2 garlic cloves, peeled

1½ teaspoons chili powder

3 cups (720 ml) low-sodium
chicken broth

½ cup (120 ml) water

2 Tablespoons lime juice

2 (425 g) cans black beans,
rinsed and drained

In a large skillet, warm olive oil over medium-low heat. Add onions and garlic and cook until softened, about 8 minutes. Add chili powder and cook 1 minute. Add broth, water, lime juice, black beans, and cooked onion mixture to the Vitamix container in the order listed and secure the lid. Select Variable 1 or the Hot Soups program. Start the machine, slowly increase to its highest speed, and blend for 6 minutes 30 seconds; or start the machine and allow the Hot Soups program to complete.

Amount Per 1 Cup (240 ml) Serving:
Calories 230, Total Fat 9g, Saturated Fat 1.5g,
Cholesterol 0mg, Sodium 75mg, Total Carbohydrate
27g, Dietary Fiber 8g, Sugars 1g, Protein 12g

"

It is so nice to be able to throw the leftover roasted vegetables from dinner into the Vitamix [blender], add broth, push a button and have soup for the following day's lunch!

– daylilydi, Polson, MT

Cauliflower Soup

(64) / *Serves 8* / *Total Time: 15 minutes*

---

3 cups (720 ml) vegetable broth

1 Tablespoon olive oil

½ teaspoon salt

½ cup (65 g) leeks, white parts
only, cleaned and cut

1½ cups (205 g) raw cashews

½ head cauliflower florets
(455 g), steamed and cooled
to room temperature

Smoked paprika, for garnish

Add broth, olive oil, salt, leeks, cashews,
and cauliflower to the Vitamix
container in the order
listed and secure the lid. Select
Variable 1 or the Hot Soups program.
Start the machine, slowly increase
to its highest speed, and blend for
6 minutes 30 seconds; or start the
machine and allow the Hot Soups
program to complete. Divide soup
among serving bowls and garnish with
smoked paprika.

Amount Per 1 Cup (240 ml) Serving:
Calories 160, Total Fat 11g, Saturated Fat 2g,
Cholesterol 0mg, Sodium 260mg, Total Carbohydrate
11g, Dietary Fiber 2g, Sugars 4g, Protein 6g

Thyme Tomato Soup

(64) / *Serves 5* / *Total Time: 15 minutes*

1½ cups (360 ml) water

1 (410 g) can diced tomatoes

2 Roma tomatoes, halved

1 medium carrot, halved

1 (2.6-ounce) jar oil-packed
sun-dried tomatoes, drained

1½ Tablespoons (15 g)
peeled and chopped onion

1 garlic clove, peeled

1½ Tablespoons chopped
fresh thyme leaves

1 teaspoon chopped fresh
oregano leaves

1 Tablespoon tomato paste

½ vegetable bouillon cube

½ teaspoon flax meal

½ cup (120 ml) whole milk,
unsweetened plain almond milk,
or rice milk, room temperature

Add all ingredients to the Vitamix
container and secure the lid. Select
Variable 1 or the Hot Soups program.
Start the machine, slowly increase
to its highest speed, and blend for
6 minutes 30 seconds; or start the
machine and allow the Hot Soups
program to complete.

Amount Per 1 Cup (240 ml) Serving:
Calories 70, Total Fat 2.5g, Saturated Fat 0g,
Cholesterol 0mg, Sodium 350mg, Total Carbohydrate
11g, Dietary Fiber 3g, Sugars 3g, Protein 2g

Mirepoix

(64) / *Makes 4 cups*
Total Time: 5 minutes

---

1 large onion (220 g), quartered

3 carrots (230 g), quartered

1 celery stalk (115 g), quartered

Add all ingredients to the Vitamix container in the order listed and add water until the ingredients float above the blades. Secure the lid. Select Variable 6 and Pulse 10 times. Drain well before use.

Chopped Cabbage

(64) / *Makes 4 1/2 cups*
Total Time: 5 minutes

---

4 cups (430 g) sliced cabbage, cut into 1-inch pieces

Add cabbage to the Vitamix container. Add water until the cabbage floats above the blades. Secure the lid. Select Variable 7 and Pulse 10 times. Drain well before use.

Fresh Sauerkraut Salad

(64) / *Makes 2 quarts*
Total Time: 40 minutes

---

1 small to medium cabbage (3 pounds / 1.2 kg), cut into small wedges

1 Tablespoon olive oil

1 medium onion (70 g), peeled and diced

1¼ cups (300 ml) cider vinegar

½ cup (120 ml) apple cider

½ cup (120 ml) water

1 Tablespoon salt

Add half of the cabbage to the Vitamix container and cover with enough water so the cabbage floats above the blades. Secure the lid and select Variable 3. Pulse 4 to 5 times. Drain and set aside. Repeat with remaining cabbage and set aside. In a large pot, warm the oil over medium heat. Add onion and sauté, stirring constantly, until it is soft and translucent. Add cider vinegar, apple cider, water, and salt to the Vitamix container and secure the lid. Select Variable 1, start the machine, and slowly increase speed to Variable 5. Blend for 15 seconds. Add the blended mixture to the sautéed onion. Add the chopped cabbage and bring the mixture to a boil. Cover and simmer 30 to 45 minutes, until the cabbage is tender. Store leftovers refrigerated in an airtight container for up to 2 weeks.

Chopped Cheese

64 / *Makes 2 cups (270 g)*
Total Time: 5 minutes

**2 cups (270 g) cubed
hard cheese**

Add cheese to the Vitamix
container and secure the lid.
Select Variable 1, start the
machine, and slowly increase
to its highest speed. Blend for
10 seconds, or until desired
consistency is reached.

Chopped Walnuts

64 / *Makes 1/3 cup (200 g)*
Total Time: 5 minutes

---

2 cups (210 g) walnuts

Add walnuts to the Vitamix
container and secure the lid.
Select Variable 5 and Pulse
10 times, or until desired
consistency is reached.

Chopped
Fresh Herbs

64 / *Makes 3/4 cup (20 g)*
Total Time: 5 minutes

**2 cups (20 g), lightly packed
fresh herb leaves**

Add herbs to the Vitamix
container and secure the lid.
Select Variable 10 and Pulse 5
to 8 times. Stop and scrape
the sides of the container.
Pulse 4 times, or until desired
consistency is reached.

Basic Vinaigrette

64 **48** / *Makes 2 1/4 cups (540 ml)*
Total Time: 10 minutes

½ cup (120 ml) red wine vinegar

2 teaspoons Dijon-style mustard

½ teaspoon ground black pepper

½ – 1 teaspoon kosher salt

1½ cups (360 ml) olive oil

½ cup (10 g) fresh herb blend

Add vinegar, mustard, pepper, and salt to the Vitamix container in the order listed and secure the lid. Select Variable 1, start the machine, and slowly increase speed to Variable 3. Blend for 10 seconds. Remove the lid plug and slowly drizzle olive oil through the lid plug opening. Add herbs through the lid plug opening and blend for 10 seconds.

Amount Per 2 Tablespoon (30 ml)
Serving: Calories 160, Total Fat 18g, Saturated Fat 2.5g, Cholesterol 0mg, Sodium 70mg, Total Carbohydrate 0g, Dietary Fiber 0g, Sugars 0g, Protein 0g

Tahini Lemon Dressing

64 **48** / *Makes 2 cups (480 ml)*
Total Time: 10 minutes

½ cup (120 ml) water

½ cup (120 ml) extra virgin olive oil

3 Tablespoons olive oil

½ cup (120 ml) tahini

½ cup (120 ml) lemon juice

2 teaspoons agave

1 teaspoon sea salt

¼ cup (6 g) fresh mint leaves

¼ cup (6 g) fresh cilantro leaves

1 garlic clove, peeled

Add all ingredients to the Vitamix container in the order listed and secure the lid. Select Variable 1, start the machine, and slowly increase to its highest speed. Blend for 30 seconds.

Amount Per 2 Tablespoon (30 ml)
Serving: Calories 130, Total Fat 14g, Saturated Fat 2g, Cholesterol 0mg, Sodium 150mg, Total Carbohydrate 3g, Dietary Fiber 0g, Sugars 1g, Protein 1g

> *I quit buying salad dressing at the grocery store because the dressings I make with my Vitamix [blender] are much tastier.*
>
> *–rdbac, Dixon, CA*

Strawberry Vinaigrette

64 / *Makes 2 1/2 cups (600 ml)*
Total Time: 10 minutes

3¾ Tablespoons red wine vinegar

3 Tablespoons lemon juice

1½ garlic cloves, peeled

9 – 12 fresh chive sprigs

10 – 12 fresh basil leaves

4 – 6 fresh parsley leaves

¾ teaspoon salt

1½ teaspoons ground
black pepper

1½ pounds (700 g) fresh
strawberries, stemmed

Add all ingredients to the
Vitamix container in the order
listed and secure the lid. Select
Variable 1, start the machine, and
slowly increase to its highest
speed. Blend for 35 seconds.

Amount Per 2 Tablespoon (30 ml)
Serving: Calories 15, Total Fat 0g,
Saturated Fat 0g, Cholesterol 0mg, Sodium
90mg, Total Carbohydrate 3g, Dietary
Fiber 1g, Sugars 2g, Protein 0g

Formula for
Homemade Vinaigrettes

Vinaigrettes are so easy to make, and so adaptable for your favorite flavor profiles. The basic formula is:

OLIVE OIL + ACID + SALT + AROMATICS

Acids

*Citrus juice or zest
(lemon, lime, grapefruit)*

*Flavored vinegar
(balsamic, white wine,
apple cider)*

Aromatics

*Garlic, Onion,
Ginger, Celery, Carrot,
Shallots, Chives*

Storing Greens
for a Longer Life

To store greens for
maximum life, cut off
the base of the lettuce
head to loosen up
leaves. Then rinse and
wrap in paper towel,
before placing them
in a plastic bag.

Fresh herb greens
can be trimmed and
placed in a glass of
water, and left on
the counter.

Combine about 3 parts oil to 1 part
acid. If using sweeter acids, like balsamic
vinegar, less oil will be needed. Once you're
comfortable with the basic formula, you can
kick up the flavor with more robust ingredients,
like red pepper flakes, spicy mustard, or
hot sauce. Also try smoothing out the texture
with a bit of yogurt, crème fraiche,
sour cream, or buttermilk.

Batters, Dough + Whole Grain Flours

As a child, my alarm clock was the grinding of wheat in the Vitamix [blender] as my mother began making breakfast. Not being a morning person, I cozied up in bed and waited for the rich, delicious aroma of freshly ground wheat pancakes filled with apples or blueberries to make its way down the hall and into my bedroom. What a wonderful way to begin the day. Thanks, Mom!

Christy Hooper,
Fourth generation

Batters, Dough +
Whole Grain Flours

Waffle Batter

 64 / *Makes 10 waffles* / *Total Time: 25 minutes*

1 cup (120 g) whole wheat flour

1 cup (125 g) all-purpose flour

1 Tablespoon baking powder

1 teaspoon salt

2 cups (480 ml) low-fat or soy milk

2 large eggs, beaten, or ½ cup
(120 ml) egg substitute

2 Tablespoons (30 ml) honey
or granulated sugar

4 ounces (110 g) soft tofu

Combine flours, baking powder, and salt in a medium-size mixing bowl and set aside. Add milk, eggs, sugar, and tofu to the Vitamix container in the order listed and secure the lid. Select Variable 1, start the machine, and slowly increase to its highest speed. Blend for 20 seconds. Reduce the speed to Variable 4 and remove the lid plug. Slowly add the flour mixture through the lid plug opening and blend for 10 seconds. Let batter sit for 5 to 10 minutes before cooking for best texture and flavor.

Amount Per 1 Waffle Serving: Calories 175, Total Fat 3g, Saturated Fat 1g, Cholesterol 62mg, Sodium 526mg, Total Carbohydrate 30g, Dietary Fiber 2g, Sugars 7g, Protein 8g

*

Get Creative with Waffle Irons

Waffles aren't the only thing waffle irons are good for. Try muffin batter, frittata mixtures, shredded hashbrowns or even sliced apples or peaches.

Bran Cherry Muffins

_____

- ½ cups whole wheat flour
- Tablespoon baking powder
- Tablespoon baking soda
- ¼ teaspoon sea salt
- ¼ cups skim milk
- Tablespoons plain 0% Greek yogurt
- 2 large eggs
- ⅓ cup molasses
- teaspoon ground cinnamon
- ¼ teaspoon ground ginger
- Tablespoon light brown sugar
- ½ cups wheat bran
- ¼ cup chopped almonds
- ⅓ cup unsweetened dried cherries

Preheat oven to 350°F (175°C). Lightly coat a mini-muffin pan with cooking spray or add paper liners. In a small bowl, combine flour, baking powder, baking soda, and salt, and set aside. Add milk, yogurt, eggs, molasses, spices, brown sugar, and bran to the Vitamix container in the order listed and secure the lid. Select Variable 1, start the machine, and slowly increase to its highest speed. Blend for 15 seconds.

Add the dry ingredients to the Vitamix container and secure the lid. Select Variable 7. Pulse 6 to 8 times to incorporate. Remove the lid and stir in the almonds and cranberries. Let sit for 10 minutes before scooping into prepared muffin tin. Bake for 10 to 12 minutes, or until a toothpick inserted in the center comes out clean.

Amount Per 1 Muffin (44 g) Serving: Calories 100, Total Fat 3g, Saturated Fat 0g, Cholesterol 15mg, Sodium 130mg, Total Carbohydrate 17g, Dietary Fiber 3g, Sugars 8g, Protein 4g

> "
>
> *I make my own wheat flour from raw ingredients. My children love my bread AND it's healthy for them! Even simple sandwiches are a win in my house.*
>
> – Mercedez

Whole Wheat Pizza Dough

(64) / *Makes 1 Large Pizza Crust*
Total Time: 35 minutes

---

3 cups unbleached whole wheat flour

1¾ teaspoons instant fast rise yeast

1¼ teaspoons salt

3¾ teaspoons olive oil

1 cup (240 ml) hot water

Preheat oven to 425°F (220°C). Lightly grease
a large mixing bowl and a pizza pan and
set aside. Add flour, yeast, and salt to the
Vitamix container and secure the lid. Select
Variable 1, start the machine, and slowly
increase speed to Variable 8. Blend for 5
seconds. Stop machine and remove the lid
plug. Select Variable 3 and quickly Pulse
about 60 times, while slowly adding oil and
water through the lid plug opening. After a
ball has formed, Pulse continuously for 5
to 10 seconds. With floured hands, remove
the dough and form into a round ball. Place
dough in prepared mixing bowl, turning over
to grease on all sides. Let rise for 10 minutes.
Stretch onto pizza pan and top with desired
toppings. Bake for 12 to 15 minutes.

Amount Per 1 Slice (80 g) Serving: Calories 170, Total
Fat 3.5g, Saturated Fat 0g, Cholesterol 0mg, Sodium 370mg,
Total Carbohydrate 33g, Dietary Fiber 5g, Sugars 0g, Protein 6g

Whole Grain Corn Bread

(64) (48) / *Makes 1 Loaf*
Total Time: 35 minutes

1½ cups (213 g) whole grain yellow cornmeal

1 cup (137 g) whole wheat flour

1 teaspoon baking powder

1 teaspoon kosher salt

½ teaspoon baking soda

1½ cups (360 ml) nonfat buttermilk

¼ cup (60 ml) canola oil

2 large eggs

3 Tablespoons (44 g) unsalted butter

1 Tablespoon honey

Place a 10-inch (25.5-cm) cast iron skillet in
the oven. Preheat oven to 425°F (220°C). In
a large bowl, combine cornmeal, flour, baking
powder, salt, and baking soda, and set aside.
Add buttermilk, oil, eggs, butter, and honey to the
Vitamix container in the order listed and secure
the lid. Select Variable 1, start the machine, and
slowly increase to its highest speed. Blend for
15 seconds. Pour the blended mixture into the
dry ingredients and stir to combine. Carefully
remove preheated skillet from the oven, and
pour batter into the pan. Bake for 20 minutes,
or until browned on edges and lightly browned
on top. Cool 5 minutes before slicing.

Amount Per 1 Square (60 g) Serving: Calories 140, Total
Fat 7g, Saturated Fat 2g, Cholesterol 30mg, Sodium 230mg,
Total Carbohydrate 16g, Dietary Fiber 2g, Sugars 2g, Protein 3g

Spinach Pasta Dough

(64) / *Makes 0.7 pounds (11 ounces)*
Total Time: 9 hours

2 large eggs

2 Tablespoons (30 ml) olive oil

3 cups (90 g) spinach, blanched

1½ cups (190 g) all-purpose flour + extra for rolling

1 teaspoon salt

¼ teaspoon ground black pepper

Add eggs, olive oil, and spinach to the Vitamix container and secure the lid. Select Variable 1. Start the machine and slowly increase to its highest speed. Blend for 20 seconds. Remove the lid and add the flour, salt, and pepper. Secure the lid and select Variable 3. Pulse 5 to 6 times until the dough starts to form a ball and lift off the blades. Remove the lid and scrape down the sides, adding a little flour if the dough looks too moist and it has not formed a ball. Pulse again 5 to 6 times. Remove from container onto a floured work surface and knead for 1 to 2 minutes. Wrap in plastic wrap and let rest for 30 minutes. Cut dough into four pieces.

One piece at a time, while the others are still wrapped, run through a pasta rolling machine, starting on the widest setting and slowly working your way down to the second to last setting. Use the pasta rolling machine's fettuccini attachment to cut the pasta into strips. Place strips on a drying rack and allow to dry overnight. Repeat with remaining dough.

Amount Per 1/4 Cup (2 ounce)
Serving: Calories 200, Total Fat 7g, Saturated Fat 1.5g, Cholesterol 70mg, Sodium 470mg, Total Carbohydrate 28g, Dietary Fiber 2g, Sugars 0g, Protein 6g

"

*I used the Dry
Grains Container and
made an oat flour recipe.
It took a couple of seconds
and I didn't need to drive
to town for oat flour.*

*–Gary and Susan,
Steamboat Springs, CO*

*

If using the 48-ounce container, reduce the ingredients to 2 cups

Whole Grain Flours

64 / *Makes 3 1/2 cups (700 g)*
Total Time: 5 minutes

Whole Wheat Flour:

3 cups (610 g) whole wheat kernels

Brown Rice Flour:

3 cups (500 g) long grain brown rice, uncooked

Cornmeal:

3 cups (500 g) raw popcorn kernels (unpopped)

Add desired flour ingredient to the Vitamix container and secure the lid. Select Variable 1, start the machine, and slowly increase to its highest speed. Blend for 35 seconds.

Grinding Whole Grains

01. Place up to 3 cups (500 g) whole kernel grain into the Vitamix container and secure the lid. Select Variable 1.

02. Start machine and slowly increase to its highest speed.

03. Process for up to 1 minute, using the tamper to press the grains toward the blades; the longer you blend, the finer your flour.

04. Store flour at room temperature for up to 1 month, refrigerated for up to 2 months, or frozen for 6 to 12 months. Bring flour to room temperature before use.

You'll yield about 1/2 cup more flour than the amount of whole grains you started with.

Baby Food

At one particular demonstration, a frustrated mother vocalized that her toddler would never drink the smoothie full of fruits and vegetables. It was suggested that the smoothie be put into the sippy cup the little girl was gripping at the time. Not only did her daughter like the green smoothie, but she refused to let the cup go. Here's to your health, little one.

Jodi Berg,
President & CEO

Fourth generation

Baby Food

Mix + Match
Baby Food

*

*Rinse canned
vegetables
thoroughly
before
blending to
reduce sodium
content*

01.

Fruit:

2 cups (about 300 g)
fresh or frozen
unsweetened, thawed:

Ripe peach, pitted
and peeled

Ripe mango, peeled,
halved, and pitted

Avocado, halved,
pitted, and peeled

Apple, peeled,
seeded, and steamed

Ripe banana, peeled

Papaya, peeled,
quartered, and seeded

Ripe pear, peeled,
seeded, and steamed

02.

Vegetables:

2 cups (about 300 g)
fresh, frozen, or canned*
vegetable, cooked:

Sweet potatoes, peeled

Peas

Winter squash,
peeled and seeded

Carrots

Green beans

Spinach

Corn

03.

Meat:

2 cups (about 280 g)
boneless meat, cubed
and cooked:

Chicken

Turkey

Pork

Beef

Veal

Lamb

Blend.

Add ½ cup (120 ml)
water, formula, breast
milk, or cooking liquid to
the Vitamix container.

Add 2 cups of selected
ingredients to the
container and firmly
secure the lid. Select
Variable 1, start the
machine, and slowly
increase speed to
Variable 6.

Increase speed as
needed, depending on
ingredients used and
desired consistency.

Blend for 20 to 30
seconds. If mixture is too
thick, remove lid plug
and add ¼ cup (60 ml)
liquid at a time through
the lid plug opening until
ingredients flow freely
through the blades.

Secure the lid plug and
continue blending until
desired consistency is
reached.

Serve immediately or
freeze leftover baby food
in ice cube trays.

Apple Pear Purée ⑨

(64) (48) / *Serves 12*
Total Time: 15 minutes

___

2 apples, cored and quartered

2 pears, cored and quartered

½ cup (120 ml) water

Combine fruit and water in a microwavable bowl and cover with plastic wrap. Steam in the microwave for about 5 minutes, until the fruit is very tender, and let cool. Place soft fruit and reserved liquid into the Vitamix container and secure the lid. Select Variable 1 or the Dips + Spreads program. Start the machine, slowly increase to its highest speed, and blend for 1 minute; or start the machine and allow the Dips + Spreads program to complete.

Amount Per 1/4 Cup (60 ml) Serving:
Calories 40, Total Fat 0g, Saturated Fat 0g, Cholesterol 0mg, Sodium 30mg, Total Carbohydrate 10g, Dietary Fiber 2g, Sugars 7g, Protein 0g

Sweet Potato Purée

(64) (48) / *Serves 6*
Total Time: 15 minutes

___

½ cup (120 ml) skim milk

1 large sweet potato, about 1 pound (450 g), baked and peeled

Add all ingredients to the Vitamix container and secure the lid. Select Variable 1, start the machine, and slowly increase to its highest speed. Blend for 30 seconds, using the tamper to press ingredients toward the blades.

Amount Per 1/4 Cup (60 ml) Serving:
Calories 60, Total Fat 0g, Saturated Fat 0g, Cholesterol 0mg, Sodium 30mg, Total Carbohydrate 14g, Dietary Fiber 2g, Sugars 5g, Protein 2g

Top 5 Baby Food Spices

Cinnamon: Blend with apples, bananas, pears, apricots, sweet potatoes, baked goods, oatmeal, brown rice cereal, and yogurt.

Cloves: Add to carrots, sweet potatoes, roasted root vegetables, apples, pears, figs, oatmeal, and brown rice cereal.

Cardamom: Can be added to apples, pears, apricots, yogurt, plums, squash, rice, and carrots.

Curry: Works well with apples, lentils, carrots, sweet potatoes, tofu, beans, pumpkin, squash, and kale.

Cumin: Adds dimension to beans, rice, carrots, lentils, sweet potatoes, roasted potatoes, broccoli, and spinach.

Add enough of the reserved steaming liquid, breast milk, or formula to thin the purée to a consistency your baby can handle.

Refrigerate in an airtight container for up to 3 days, or spoon individual portions into ice cube trays and freeze, covered, for up to 3 months.

Desserts

I loved watching Vitamix demonstrators flip the container upside down to show audiences how frozen ice cream gets. Making peanut butter ice cream for my friends, I hesitated, but couldn't resist. I held the container high above my head, and was mortified as the slightly melted ice cream refused to grip the sides of the container and slid down my face and onto the floor.

Molli Dieterich,

Fifth generation

Desserts

Strawberry Spiced Vegan Ice Cream

(64) (48) / *Serves 6*
Total Time: 10 minutes

1 cup (240 ml) plain unsweetened almond milk

½ jalapeño pepper

¼ cup (35 g) coconut sugar

3 cups (370 g) frozen strawberries

Add all ingredients to the Vitamix container in the order listed and secure the lid. Select Variable 1, start the machine, and slowly increase to its highest speed. Blend for 35 to 40 seconds, using the tamper to press ingredients toward the blades. Serve immediately.

Amount Per 1/2 Cup (120 ml) Serving:
Calories 60, Total Fat 0.5g, Saturated Fat 0g, Cholesterol 0mg, Sodium 30mg, Total Carbohydrate 15g, Dietary Fiber 2g, Sugars 11g, Protein 0g

Peach Soy Sherbet (®)

(64) / *Serves 10*
Total Time: 5 minutes

1½ cups (360 ml) plain unsweetened soy milk

3 Tablespoons (45 ml) honey

1 teaspoon vanilla extract

1½ pounds (680 g) frozen peach slices

Add all ingredients to the Vitamix container in the order listed and secure the lid. Select Variable 1 or the Frozen Desserts Program. Start the machine, slowly increase to its highest speed, and blend for 55 seconds; or start the machine and allow the Frozen Desserts program to complete. Use the tamper to press ingredients toward the blades.

Amount Per 1/2 Cup (120 ml) Serving:
Calories 60, Total Fat 0.5g, Saturated Fat 0g, Cholesterol 0mg, Sodium 20mg, Total Carbohydrate 14g, Dietary Fiber 1g, Sugars 11g, Protein 2g

*

How to Make Frozen Desserts

A frozen dessert in your Vitamix blender can be as easy as a couple frozen bananas, with a couple drops of vanilla if you want to get fancy. These desserts are so simple and need no added sweeteners to make them feel decadent. Here are a few simple tips to get a perfect dessert, every time.

1. **Crank up the speed.** For thick and frozen blends, use your blender's highest speed setting. You'll need the power to cut through frozen ingredients.

2. **Use the tamper.** You'll need to keep pressing the ingredients toward the blades for a smooth, even blend. Think of it as your arm workout for the day.

3. **Don't overdo it.** Blending for more than a minute will cause the mixture to start melting. Plus, the faster it's made, the faster you can enjoy a spoonful.

4. **Make it your own.** The ideal ratio for frozen desserts is 1 cup frozen to ¼ cup liquid. Stick to that ratio, and you won't end up with a smoothie when you wanted an ice cream.

Mango Basil Frozen Yogurt

64 48 / *Serves 8*
Total Time: 15 minutes

2 cups (285 g) fresh ripe
mango, rough chopped

1 Tablespoon honey or maple syrup

1 cup (215 g) Greek yogurt

2 Tablespoons chopped fresh basil

1 teaspoon lime zest

2 cups (285 g) frozen mango chunks

1 cup (130 g) ice cubes

In a medium-size bowl, stir together
the fresh mango pieces and honey.
Set aside and let sit at room
temperature for 10 minutes. Add
yogurt, mango and honey mixture,
basil, zest, frozen mango, and ice
cubes to the Vitamix container
in the order listed and secure
the lid. Select Variable 1 or the
Frozen Desserts program. Start
the machine, slowly increase to
its highest speed, and blend for 55
seconds; or start the machine and
allow the Frozen Desserts program
to complete. Use the tamper to press
the ingredients toward the blades.

Amount Per 1/2 Cup (120 ml) Serving:
Calories 80, Total Fat 0.5g, Saturated Fat
0g, Cholesterol 0mg, Sodium 10mg, Total
Carbohydrate 17g, Dietary Fiber 2g,
Sugars 16g, Protein 3g

Vanilla Ice Cream

64 48 / *Serves 10*
Total Time: 5 minutes

1 cup (240 ml) whole milk

28 whole milk ice cubes

1 cup (120 g) powdered sugar

1 Tablespoon vanilla extract
(optional)

Add all ingredients to the Vitamix
container in the order listed and
secure the lid. Select Variable 1, start
the machine, and slowly increase
to its highest speed. Blend for 30
seconds, using the tamper to press
ingredients toward the blades.

Amount Per 1/2 Cup (120 ml) Serving:
Calories 110, Total Fat 3.5g, Saturated Fat
2g, Cholesterol 10mg, Sodium 45mg, Total
Carbohydrate 17g, Dietary Fiber 0g,
Sugars 17g, Protein 3g

> I make banana
> ice cream using frozen
> bananas and water
> and this is the only
> product that I have
> been able to reach the
> desired consistency.
>
> –*Banana Girl, Ohio*

Ginger Peach Granita 🌲

64 **48** / *Serves 5*
Total Time: 3 hours

---

2 large peaches (375 g), pitted

1 Tablespoon (10 g) peeled and chopped fresh ginger root

1 cup (240 ml) simple syrup

1 Tablespoon lemon juice

1 cup (240 ml) water

Add all ingredients to the Vitamix container in the order listed and secure the lid. Select Variable 1 or the Frozen Desserts program. Start the machine, slowly increase to its highest speed, and blend for 55 seconds; or start the machine and allow the Frozen Desserts program to complete. Pour into a shallow pan or sheet tray and place in the freezer. Every 30 minutes, use a fork to fluff the mixture. Freeze for at least 3 hours, or up to overnight.

Amount Per 1 Cup (240 ml) Serving:
Calories 370, Total Fat 0g, Saturated Fat 0g, Cholesterol 0mg, Sodium 0mg, Total Carbohydrate 95g, Dietary Fiber 1g, Sugars 94g, Protein 1g

Whipped Cream

  / *Makes 2 cups*
Total Time: 5 minutes

2 cups (480 ml) heavy
whipping cream

Add cream to the Vitamix
container and secure the lid. Select
Variable 1, start the machine, and
slowly increase to its highest
speed. Blend for 3o to 45 seconds.

Amount Per 2 Tablespoon (30 ml)
Serving: Calories 50, Total Fat 6g,
Saturated Fat 3.5g, Cholesterol 20mg,
Sodium 5mg, Total Carbohydrate 0g, Dietary
Fiber 0g, Sugars 0g, Protein 0g

Chocolate Sauce

  / *Serves 14*
Total Time: 15 minutes

2½ cups (600 ml) cashew milk

⅔ cup (55 g) unsweetened
cocoa powder

1 cup (140 g) dried pitted dates

6 ounces (170 g)
bittersweet chocolate

1½ teaspoons vanilla extract

Add all ingredients to the
Vitamix container in the order
listed and secure the lid. Select
Variable 1, start the machine, and
slowly increase to its highest
speed. Blend for 2 minutes 30
seconds, using the tamper as
needed, until the mixture is
smooth and warm.

Amount Per 1/4 Cup (60 ml)
Serving: Calories 110, Total Fat 6g,
Saturated Fat 3g, Cholesterol 0mg,
Sodium 30mg, Total Carbohydrate 18g,
Dietary Fiber 4g, Sugars 13g, Protein 2g

Powdered Sugar

  / *Makes 2 cups*
Total Time: 5 minutes

1½ cups (300 g) granulated sugar

1 Tablespoon cornstarch

Add sugar to the Vitamix
container and secure the lid.
Select Variable 1, start the
machine, and slowly increase
to its highest speed. Blend for
30 seconds. Reduce speed to
Variable 3 and remove the lid
plug. Add cornstarch through
the lid plug opening and
secure the lid plug. Slowly return
to the highest speed and blend
for 10 seconds.

Amount Per 1 Teaspoon (5 g) Serving:
Calories 10, Total Fat 0g, Saturated Fat
0g, Cholesterol 0mg, Sodium 0mg, Total
Carbohydrate 2g, Dietary Fiber 0g,
Sugars 2g, Protein 0g

*

Finishing Touches: Flavored Whipped Cream

You can use the simple syrup ideas from the Coffee + Milkshake section, or blend whole ingredients into the basic Whipped Cream recipe. Add a teaspoon or two of chocolate or caramel sauce, chopped nuts, spices like cinnamon and nutmeg, herbs like mint, espresso powder, or peanut butter. Tip: Just be careful not to overmix, or the cream will turn to butter. Ten seconds of blending should do it.

Cocoa Pudding

(64) (48) / *Serves 8*
Total Time: 12 hours

1¼ cups (300 ml) almond milk

2 Tablespoons coconut milk

1 Tablespoon maple syrup

¼ cup (24 g) unsweetened
cocoa powder

2 Tablespoons (20 g) chia seeds

⅛ teaspoon Himalayan
or Celtic salt

½ teaspoon vanilla extract

Add all ingredients to the
Vitamix container in the order
listed and secure the lid. Select
Variable 1, start the machine,
and slowly increase to its highest
speed. Blend for 45 seconds.
Pour blended mixture into a
bowl, cover, and refrigerate
overnight to thicken.

Amount Per 1/4 Cup (60 ml) Serving
Calories 45, Total Fat 2g, Saturated Fat
0g, Cholesterol 0mg, Sodium 75mg, Total
Carbohydrate 6g, Dietary Fiber 2g,
Sugars 3g, Protein 1g

Chia Pudding

(64) (48) / *Serves 4*
Total Time: 12 hours

1½ cups (360 ml) coconut milk

¾ cup (275 ml) plain Greek yogurt

1 Tablespoon honey

1 teaspoon vanilla extract

⅓ cup (60 g) chia seeds

Pinch of salt

For Garnish:

2 ounces (40 g) dark
chocolate, chopped

⅓ cup (50 g) toasted almonds

Add coconut milk, yogurt, honey,
vanilla, chia seeds, and salt to
the Vitamix container in the order
listed and secure the lid. Select
Variable 1, start the machine, and
slowly increase to its highest
speed. Blend for 45 seconds.
Transfer to a bowl and refrigerate,
covered, overnight. To serve,
divide pudding into 4 glasses and
top with chocolate and almonds.

Amount Per 1/4 Cup (60 ml) Serving
Calories 290, Total Fat 23g, Saturated Fat
17g, Cholesterol 5mg, Sodium 105mg, Total
Carbohydrate 14g, Dietary Fiber 5g,
Sugars 6g, Protein 8g

Carrot Cake

 48 / *Serves 12* / *Total Time: 1 hour*

3 large eggs

6 Tablespoons (100 g) applesauce

1 Tablespoon vanilla extract

½ cup (120 ml) low-fat buttermilk

1 cup (150 g) pitted dates

½ cup (50 g) brown sugar

1 cup (150 g) whole wheat flour

1½ cups (200 g) all-purpose flour

2 teaspoons (5 g) ground cinnamon

2 Tablespoons (25 g) baking powder

2 cups (300 g) chopped carrots

Preheat oven to 350°F (175°C). Grease a 9-inch (23-cm) spring form pan with cooking spray and set aside. Add eggs, applesauce, vanilla, buttermilk, dates, and brown sugar to the Vitamix container and secure the lid. Select Variable 1, start the machine, and slowly increase to its highest speed. Blend for 1 minute. In a large-size bowl, stir together flours, cinnamon, baking powder, and carrots. Pour blended mixture into the dry ingredients and stir to combine. Pour batter into prepared pan and bake for 30 minutes, or until a toothpick inserted into the center comes out clean. Serve warm or at room temperature.

Amount Per 1 Slice Serving: Calories 210, Total Fat 2g, Saturated Fat 0.5g, Cholesterol 45mg, Sodium 290mg, Total Carbohydrate 44g, Dietary Fiber 4g, Sugars 21g, Protein 5g

Notes:

* *Notes:*